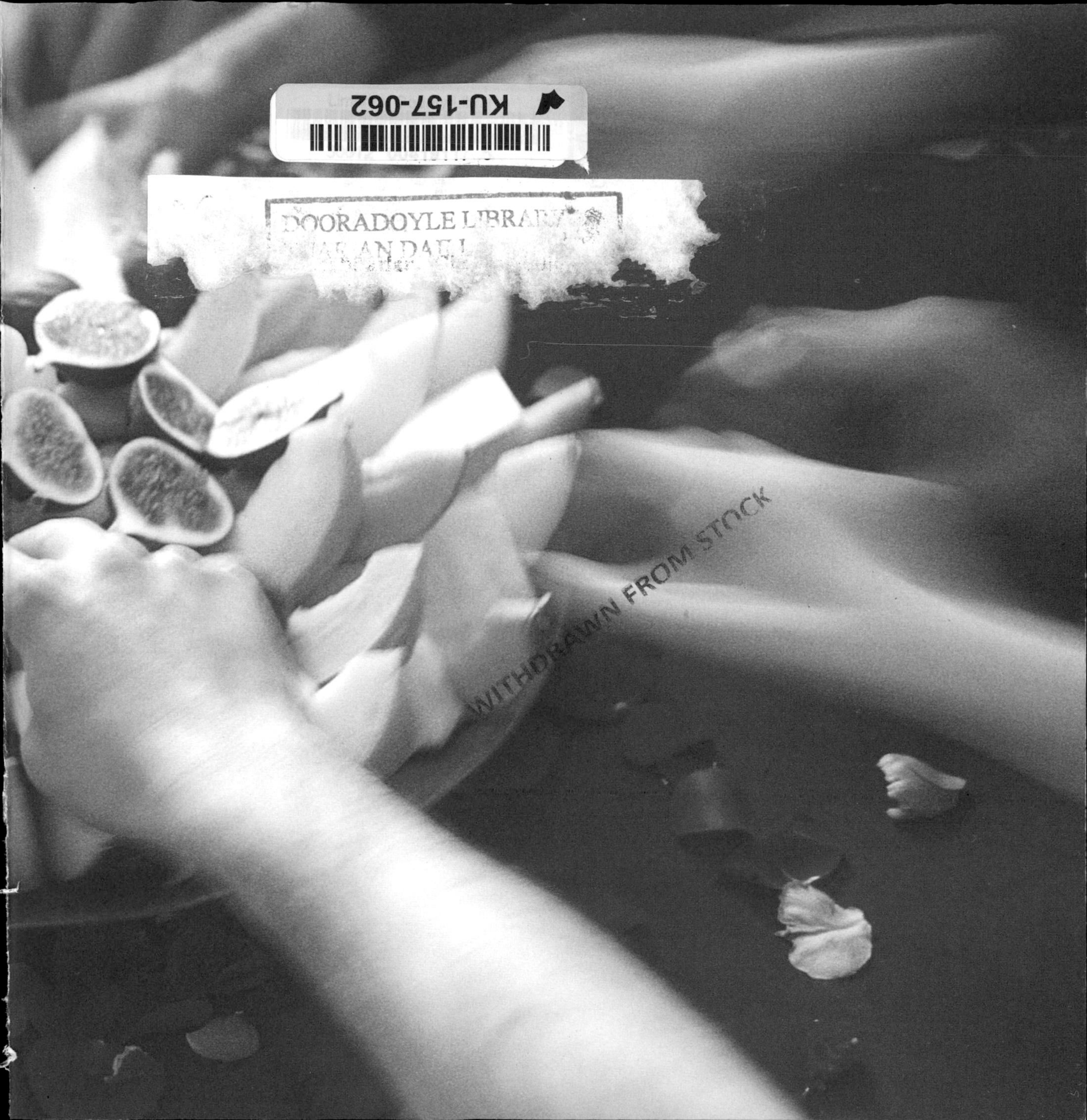

PARTY!

PARTY!

EASY RECIPES FOR FINGERFOOD AND PARTY DRINKS

Fran Warde   Photography by Debi Treloar

RYLAND
PETERS
& SMALL

LONDON NEW YORK

First published in Great Britain in 2003
by Ryland Peters & Small
Kirkman House
12–14 Whitfield Street
London W1T 2RP
www.rylandpeters.com

10 9 8 7 6 5 4 3 2 1

Text © Fran Warde 2003
Design and photographs
© Ryland Peters & Small 2003

Printed and bound in China

ISBN 1 84172 501 3

Commissioning Editor Elsa Petersen-Schepelern
Editor Sharon Ashman
Production Louise Bartrum
Art Director Gabriella Le Grazie
Publishing Director Alison Starling

Food Stylist Fran Warde
Stylists Emily Chalmers and Helen Trent
Indexer Hilary Bird

Notes
Spoon measurements are level unless otherwise stated.
Ovens should be preheated to the specified temperature.
If using a fan-assisted oven, cooking times should be
reduced according to the manufacturer's instructions.
Specialist Asian ingredients are available in larger
supermarkets and Asian stores.
Uncooked or partly cooked eggs should not be served to
the very young, the very old or frail, or to pregnant women.

Recipes in this book have previously been published
in *Eat Drink Live* and *Food For Friends* by Fran Warde.

contents

party time

Everyone loves a party. As the host, you will want your friends to have lots of fun, but your guests will also want to see you enjoying yourself – while serving beautiful drinks and delicious food with the greatest of ease and style. This book will help you throw a party that is both enjoyable and memorable.

Food and friends go hand in hand, so if you are organizing a get-together, whatever the number of guests, you will want to serve some food. The style of party you choose to give will dictate the food you offer. So here you will find a great selection of ideas from quick, easy nibbles to serve at an impromptu gathering, to more substantial recipes for planned parties and special celebrations. There are also sweet treats – party style – and of course, great suggestions for chic cocktails that will get any party buzzing with excitement. All the recipes can be eaten standing up with nothing more than a napkin to catch the odd crumb. Even the sweet treats are small for easy handling.

The recipes in this book are simple to follow and designed not to take up too much of your precious party time. The best hosts are those who want to enjoy themselves rather than slaving in the kitchen while their guests are having all the fun. So get organized and prepare as much as possible in advance. Your friends have come to spend time with you and meet new people. If you are the best host in town, they will have great food and refreshments, a fun evening with you and maybe even take home a new telephone number or two. Get planning, inviting, shopping, cooking and then open your doors for a great party. Yes, it's that simple!

nibbles and dips

spiced nuts

Let the nuts cool before eating. They can be made the day before the party, just make sure you store them in an airtight container until needed.

1 teaspoon cumin seeds

1 teaspoon fennel seeds

1 teaspoon sweet smoked paprika

1 teaspoon flaked sea salt

2 tablespoons olive oil

100 g cashew nuts

100 g brazil nuts

100 g almonds

100 g peanuts

100 g shelled pistachios

2 baking sheets

serves 4

Crush the cumin and fennel seeds coarsely with a mortar and pestle. Transfer to a bowl and add the paprika, salt and oil. Mix well, then add all the nuts and mix again until the nuts are well coated.

Spread the nuts in an even layer on the 2 baking sheets and roast in a preheated oven at 180°C (350°F) Gas 4 for 10 minutes. Remove from the oven and turn the nuts with a spoon so they cook evenly. Return them to the oven and roast for a further 10 minutes. Remove from the oven and set aside to cool.

parmesan and rosemary wafers

These are a must for any good party. Everyone will be constantly nibbling, so make plenty. They can be made up to 2 days in advance but must be kept chilled in an airtight container.

2 sprigs of rosemary, leaves stripped and finely chopped

200 g Parmesan cheese, coarsely grated

2 baking sheets, lined with baking parchment

makes 24

Put the rosemary and Parmesan in a bowl and mix. Put teaspoons of the mixture in little heaps on the baking sheets and flatten out into circles. Make sure they are not too close because they will spread in the oven. Bake in a preheated oven at 200°C (400°F) Gas 6 for 8–10 minutes until golden. Remove from the oven and let cool. Gently peel off the paper and serve.

crispy noodles

These rice vermicelli snacks are known as *mee krob* in their homeland of Thailand. They are always popular, so be sure to make plenty for your gathering. The vegetables can be chopped in advance but the vermicelli really should be cooked at the last minute for a crispy, fresh flavour.

sunflower oil, for deep-frying and stir-frying

50 g rice vermicelli

1 onion, finely chopped

1 garlic clove, chopped

3 cm fresh ginger, peeled and chopped

1 fresh red chilli, chopped

a bunch of coriander, chopped

a bunch of chives, chopped

2 mini lettuces, such as Little Gem

makes 20

Fill a wok one-third full of oil and heat. To test if the oil is hot enough to begin cooking, add a piece of vermicelli: it should puff up immediately. If it sinks to the bottom heat the oil a little longer.

Add the vermicelli in small handfuls, turning it with tongs to help it puff up evenly, this will take 40–60 seconds. Transfer the vermicelli to a plate lined with crumpled kitchen paper. Pour the oil into a heatproof container.

Wipe out the wok and return to the heat. Add 1 tablespoon oil, then the onion, garlic, ginger and chilli. Stir-fry for 5 minutes.

Turn off the heat, add the cooked noodles to the wok and mix well. Stir in the herbs.

Break the lettuce leaves away from the stem. Fill them with spoonfuls of the noodle mixture and arrange on a plate to serve.

raw vegetable platter

A selection of fresh vegetables makes a stunning centrepiece.

8 carrots, cut into batons

8 baby fennel bulbs, trimmed and halved

1 cucumber, cut into batons

2 bunches of radishes, trimmed

8 tablespoons extra virgin olive oil

3 tablespoons balsamic vinegar

serves 12

Arrange the raw vegetables on a big serving plate. Put the oil and vinegar in a small dipping bowl and mix. Serve with the vegetables.

artichoke hoummus with ciabatta

You can make this dip the night before: just remember to remove it from the refrigerator a while before serving so the flavours can warm up. Instead of ciabatta bread, you can serve the hoummus with cheese straws, grissini (Italian breadsticks), pita, biscuits or other bread for dipping or spreading.

280 g artichoke hearts in olive oil, drained

80 g canned borlotti beans, drained

sea salt and freshly ground black pepper

to serve

ciabatta bread, toasted

cheese straws or grissini

serves 4

Put the artichoke hearts and beans in a food processor or blender and process until smooth. Transfer to a bowl and season with salt and pepper to taste. Serve the hoummus with the toasted ciabatta and cheese straws or grissini.

potato skins with green dip

The cheese can be either melted and soft or crisp and crunchy – keep checking and remove from the oven at the right moment. Save the potato flesh for another day.

12 large baking potatoes

200 ml olive oil

400 g mature Cheddar cheese, grated

green dip

400 ml sour cream

2 bunches of chives, chopped

2 bunches of spring onions, chopped

a bunch of flat leaf parsley, chopped

sea salt and freshly ground black pepper

a baking sheet, lightly oiled

serves 24

Using a small, sharp knife, pierce each potato right through the middle. Bake in a preheated oven at 180°C (350°F) Gas 4 for 1 hour 10 minutes or until cooked through. Remove and set aside until cool enough to handle. Cut each potato in half lengthways and, using a dessertspoon, scoop out the soft potato middles, leaving a thin layer lining the skin. Cut each skin half into 4 wedges, then cover and refrigerate until needed. (You can prepare the potatoes ahead to this point the day before the party.)

To make the dip, put the sour cream, chives, spring onions and parsley in a bowl. Add salt and pepper to taste and mix well.

Brush oil over the potato skins and arrange in a single layer on the oiled baking sheet. Bake at the top of a preheated oven at 220°C (425°F) Gas 7 for 30 minutes until golden, moving the potato skins around occasionally so they cook evenly. Remove from the oven and reduce the heat to 200°C (400°F) Gas 6.

Sprinkle the potato skins with cheese and return to the oven for 5–10 minutes, until the cheese is melted or crunchy, checking after 5 minutes if you want it melted. Serve with the green dip.

bread, wraps and rolls

sage and stilton flatbread

Serve this with drinks when your guests arrive. If Stilton is not your favourite cheese, try using another blue cheese such as Roquefort or Gorgonzola, or try brie or a hard cheese, such as Cheddar.

500 g plain flour

1 teaspoon baking powder

225 ml Greek yoghurt

100 g butter, melted

2 eggs, beaten

3 tablespoons chopped fresh sage

100 g Stilton cheese, crumbled

a baking sheet, lightly oiled

serves 8

Sift the flour and baking powder into a bowl and make a well in the centre. Put the yoghurt, melted butter, eggs and sage in a separate bowl and mix. Pour the yoghurt mixture into the well in the flour and stir with a wooden spoon until well blended.

Knead the dough into a ball, put on the oiled baking sheet and roll out to a circle about 30 cm diameter. Cook in a preheated oven at 180°C (350°F) Gas 4 for 20 minutes. Remove the bread from the oven, crumble the Stilton over the top and return to the oven for a further 10 minutes. Remove the bread from the oven and let cool a little. Transfer to a large chopping board, cut into wedges and serve.

grissini sticks with parma ham

It's best to buy these ingredients at an Italian delicatessen, as the grissini sticks will be skinny and crunchy, made with good flour in the traditional way, and the Parma ham can be sliced to order. Assemble these nibbles up to an hour in advance of your party.

12 very thin slices Parma ham

12 grissini (Italian breadsticks)

serves 12

Trim off the excess fat from the Parma ham and wrap a slice around the top half of each grissini. Arrange in glasses or on a large plate and serve.

garlic and parsley bread

Everyone loves this easy bread which makes ideal party food. It's at its best if you grill it at the last minute then serve it immediately, while still warm.

3–4 garlic cloves, finely chopped

a bunch of flat leaf parsley, chopped

½ teaspoon crushed dried chillies

2 loaves ciabatta bread, split lengthways

olive oil, for sprinkling

sea salt and freshly ground black pepper

serves 8

Spread the garlic, parsley, dried chillies, salt and pepper evenly over the opened bread halves. Sprinkle generously with olive oil, then cook under a preheated grill until golden. Cut the bread into chunks and serve at once.

ricepaper parcels with dipping soy

These are time-consuming but worth it, so enlist some help before the party to assemble them. They can be made up to 4 hours in advance but they must be covered with a damp cloth and clingfilm, then chilled until needed.

12 ricepaper wrappers*

2 carrots, cut into matchsticks

6 spring onions, cut into matchsticks

75 g beansprouts

leaves from a bunch of Thai basil

a bunch of watercress

1 tablespoon toasted sesame seeds

dipping soy

2 tablespoons honey

1 tablespoon soy sauce

1 tablespoon teriyaki sauce

1 red chilli, thinly sliced

serves 12

Soak the ricepaper wrappers in several changes of warm water until soft, about 4 minutes.

Gather up little clusters of the carrots, spring onions, beansprouts, basil and watercress and put a cluster in the middle of each of the softened wrappers. Sprinkle with sesame seeds and roll up to enclose the vegetables.

To make the dipping soy, put the honey, soy sauce and teriyaki sauce in a small bowl and mix. Add the chilli and transfer to a small, shallow dish to serve with the parcels.

*Note Vietnamese dried ricepaper wrappers (báhn tráng) are sold in Asian markets in quantities of 50–100. The packets they can be resealed and kept in a cool cupboard.

vegetarian mexican rolls

These are best made to order or at the last moment, otherwise the avocado will discolour. You could encourage everyone to roll their own by setting out all the fillings in bowls and leaving the avocados whole, for everyone to slice as needed.

12 large soft flour tortillas

200 g cream cheese

4 carrots, grated

a bunch of coriander, chopped

a bunch of chives, chopped

a bunch of spring onions, chopped

2 chillies, chopped

4 avocados, peeled and sliced

freshly squeezed juice of 2 lemons

4 tablespoons olive oil

sea salt and freshly ground black pepper

serves 24

Cook the tortillas according to the directions on the packet. Let cool, then put each tortilla on an individual sheet of clingfilm. Spread with the cream cheese and then sprinkle evenly with the carrot, coriander, chives, spring onions and chillies. Flatten the topping lightly with a palette knife.

Put the avocado slices in a bowl and sprinkle with lemon juice, oil, salt and pepper. Arrange over the open tortillas. Roll each tortilla into a tight cylinder, using the clingfilm to help you roll. Twist both ends in opposite directions to make a cigar shape. Chill until needed, then slice in half, with the clingfilm still on, and serve.

chicken salad wraps

Chicken is always a popular ingredient and these wraps will satisfy your hungry guests. They can be made up to 4 hours in advance and chilled until needed. If you prefer to make these into bite-sized offerings, slice each cylinder diagonally into about 8 pieces just before serving, then pierce them with a cocktail stick for easy handling.

12 soft flour tortillas, preferably wholemeal

12 tablespoons mayonnaise

6 teaspoons wholegrain mustard

6 cooked chicken breasts, shredded

6 carrots, grated

¼ white cabbage, thinly sliced

6 medium tomatoes, thinly sliced

sea salt and freshly ground black pepper

serves 12

Lay each tortilla flat on a piece of greaseproof paper. Spread with the mayonnaise and mustard.

Sprinkle with the shredded chicken, grated carrot, sliced cabbage, salt, pepper and tomato.

Roll up the tortillas into tight cylinders, using the greaseproof paper to help you. Twist the ends of the paper to secure.

To serve, cut the cylinders in half diagonally.

mexican prawn wraps

2 flour tortillas, 20 cm
diameter

salsa

1 jalapeño chilli, deseeded
and finely chopped

½ red onion, finely chopped

1 garlic clove, finely chopped

2 tomatoes, skinned,
deseeded and chopped

3 tablespoons sour cream

sea salt and freshly ground
black pepper

filling

½ avocado, peeled and sliced

freshly squeezed juice of
½ lime

75 g cooked and
peeled prawns

a small bunch of rocket,
about 50 g

makes 20

These canapés are visually stunning. The prawns can be replaced with chicken, rare beef or grated fresh vegetables such as carrots and radishes. They can be made up to 4 hours in advance, chilled, then sliced just before serving. A long, cool Mojito (page 58) is the perfect accompaniment to these wraps.

To make the salsa, put all the ingredients in a bowl and stir well.

Heat the tortillas in a dry frying pan, then transfer to a large chopping board. Divide the salsa between them and spread out evenly. Top with avocado slices and a little lime juice, then the prawns and rocket.

Roll up tightly and wrap in clingfilm, twisting the ends to secure. Chill for 30 minutes, then slice each roll into 10 pieces and arrange on a platter to serve.

goats' cheese and pepper crostini

You can bake the ficelle and assemble the crostini up to 1 hour in advance. Cover with clingfilm and chill until needed.

1 thin French breadstick (ficelle)

150 g fresh creamy goats' cheese

4 roasted red peppers, peeled

40 spears Thai asparagus, cooked and refreshed in cold water

olive oil, for brushing

sea salt and freshly ground black pepper

a baking sheet

serves 20

To make the crostini, slice the breadstick diagonally into 20 thin slices. Brush the slices with olive oil, then sprinkle with salt and pepper. Cook in a preheated oven at 190°C (375°F) Gas 5 for 5 minutes until golden.

Arrange the crostini on a plate and spread with goats' cheese. Cut the roasted peppers into thin strips, then arrange a strip of pepper and 2 spears of asparagus on each crostini. Serve.

ciabatta pizzas

Other breads can be used in these fantastic, fresh-tasting pizzas, so don't go shopping specially for ciabatta.

3 loaves ciabatta, sliced

3 garlic cloves, halved

about 12 tablespoons olive oil

12 ripe tomatoes, skinned and sliced

a handful of pitted olives

a bunch of marjoram

6 balls mozzarella cheese, drained and sliced

a bunch of basil

sea salt and freshly ground black pepper

several baking sheets

serves 12

Grill the ciabatta slices under a hot grill until lightly toasted, then rub with the cut side of the garlic. Put the garlic ciabatta on a baking sheet and sprinkle with a little olive oil.

Arrange the sliced tomatoes on the bread, then add the olives, marjoram, mozzarella, basil, salt and pepper. Sprinkle with more oil.

Cook in a preheated oven at 180°C (350°F) Gas 4 for 15–20 minutes until the mozzarella has melted. Remove from the oven, let cool and serve.

light bites

artichoke and tomato pastry boats

Using ready-rolled pastry for this recipe makes it the height of simplicity. However, preparing the delicate squares of pastry can be time-consuming so enlist some help to put these together. They can be made up to 2 hours in advance.

about 250 g ready-rolled shortcrust pastry

4 baby artichoke hearts in olive oil, drained and cut into quarters

50 g buffalo mozzarella, drained and cut into 16 pieces

8 cherry tomatoes, halved

2 spring onions, each cut into 8 pieces

1 egg yolk, lightly beaten

sea salt and freshly ground black pepper

2 baking sheets, greased

makes 16

Put the ready-rolled pastry on a lightly floured surface. Using a sharp knife, cut the pastry into 16 pieces, each measuring about 3.5 cm square. Transfer to the baking sheets.

Put a piece of artichoke, a piece of mozzarella, a tomato half and a piece of spring onion on top of each pastry square, pushing them in lightly to secure them. Brush the edges of the pastry with egg yolk, then gently squeeze the edges together to form a boat shape. Season with salt and pepper.

Bake in a preheated oven at 180°C (350°F) Gas 4 for 12–15 minutes until golden and cooked. Serve warm or at room temperature.

smoked oyster and goats' cheese pastries

I love smoked oysters and I don't think that enough people know about them, so make these delicious little pastries and let everyone enjoy. They can be made up to 4 hours in advance.

250 g ready-made puff pastry

100 g soft, rindless goats' cheese, crumbled

170 g canned smoked oysters

1 egg, beaten

sea salt and freshly ground black pepper

a baking sheet, greased

serves 12

Roll out the pastry on a lightly floured surface until very thin, to make a rectangle, then cut the pastry in half lengthways.

Put half the crumbled goats' cheese down the middle of one piece of pastry. Arrange half the oysters in a row on top of the goats' cheese. Brush the beaten egg along both the long sides, fold the pastry over lengthways and gently press the edges together to seal. Repeat with the other piece of pastry and remaining cheese and oysters.

Lightly brush both pastry parcels with beaten egg, then sprinkle with salt and pepper. Cut both parcels into 3 cm slices, then transfer to the greased baking sheet. Cook in a preheated oven at 200°C (400°F) Gas 6 for 12 minutes until puffed and golden. Let cool to room temperature before serving.

tomato and goats' cheese tart

Oh, how I love this tart – the crumbly, flaky texture of the puff pastry, the thinly sliced onions and roasted tomatoes, the melted goats' cheese binding them together. Puff pastry can be bought frozen or from the chiller cabinets. It even comes pre-rolled for the super-busy person. The tarts can be made up to 6 hours in advance, then warmed in the oven at 150°C (300°F) Gas 2 for 10 minutes if wanted hot.

375 g ready-made puff pastry

2 onions, thinly sliced

200 g baby tomatoes, roasted

150 g soft, rindless goats' cheese, crumbled

2 tablespoons olive oil

1 teaspoon caster sugar

sea salt and freshly ground black pepper

a saucer, 15 cm diameter

a baking sheet, lightly oiled

serves 4

Roll out the pastry on a lightly floured surface to about 5 mm thick and cut out 4 circles using the saucer as a template. Transfer the circles to the baking sheet. Prick the pastry all over with a fork.

Bake in a preheated oven at 190°C (375°F) Gas 5 for 15 minutes, then remove from the oven.

Put the sliced onion in a bowl with the roasted tomatoes, goats' cheese, olive oil, sugar, salt and pepper and mix well. Divide the mixture between the pastry bases, spreading it evenly over the top and pushing down gently.

Return the 4 tarts to the oven and cook for 20 minutes, then reduce the oven temperature to 180°C (350°F) Gas 4 and cook for a further 15–20 minutes until lightly browned. Serve hot or at room temperature.

chinese duck forks

These duck morsels are sweet, delicious and look wonderful. Serve them skewered on little forks, or on some Chinese porcelain spoons.

1 duck breast, skinned

3 spring onions, cut into 5 cm pieces, then thinly sliced lengthways

10 cm cucumber, peeled, deseeded, cut in half, then thinly sliced lengthways

chinese marinade

2 tablespoons soy sauce

2 tablespoons dry sherry

1 tablespoon caster sugar

2 whole star anise

5 cm fresh ginger, peeled and chopped

4 tablespoons plum sauce

12 forks or Chinese porcelain spoons

serves 12

Put all the marinade ingredients in a small non-stick pan and heat to simmering point. Add the duck breast and simmer very gently for 6 minutes on each side. Remove the pan from the heat, cover and let cool. When cool, slice the duck very thinly crossways. Reserve the marinade.

Lay out the sliced duck breast, put a few spring onion and cucumber strips at one end of each slice and roll up tightly into parcels. Push onto the forks or lay in the Chinese spoons. Sprinkle with a little of the reserved marinade and serve.

figs stuffed with parma ham

Fresh figs are irresistible, especially when they are paired with Parma ham. This is such a simple recipe but I can assure you that your guests will love it.

16 ripe figs

16 slices Parma ham

makes 16

Stand the figs upright and, using a sharp knife, cut a cross in the top of each. Put a folded slice of Parma ham inside each one. Put the stuffed figs on a serving platter and serve immediately.

Alternatively, make these up to 4 hours in advance of your party, cover them with clingfilm and chill until needed. Remove them from the refrigerator 1 hour before serving.

chicken sticks with sweet chilli

Chicken sticks are always very popular, so it's worth making extra. You can use boneless chicken thighs, but always remove any excess fat (they may also need to cook for a little longer, as the meat is denser). The skewers can be made the day before the party, just cover them with clingfilm and chill until needed. If you want to serve them hot, put them on a baking sheet and cook at 180°C (350°F) Gas 4 for 12 minutes before serving.

12 boneless, skinless chicken breasts

400 ml sweet chilli sauce

olive oil, for brushing

24 bamboo satay sticks, soaked in water for about 30 minutes

serves 24

Cut each chicken breast into 10 cubes. Put the chicken cubes in a bowl, add the sweet chilli sauce and mix well. Cover and chill overnight. When ready to cook, thread the chicken cubes onto the soaked satay sticks. Heat the grill to medium-high, then brush the rack of the grill pan with oil.

Add the chicken sticks to the rack and cook, in batches if necessary, turning frequently, for 25 minutes, or until the chicken is cooked through. Repeat until all the chicken sticks are cooked, then serve hot or cold.

honeyed chicken wings

These really should be called Last Lick Chicken Wings – anyone who eats them removes every morsel of flavour and sticky meat. Just watch out that they don't burn in the oven. They can be made the day before the party, just cover them with clingfilm and chill until needed.

16 chicken wings

200 ml runny honey

100 ml sweet chilli sauce

sea salt and freshly ground black pepper

a bunch of radishes, trimmed, to serve (optional)

serves 8

Put the chicken wings in an oiled roasting tin. Cook them in a preheated oven at 200°C (400°F) Gas 6 for 40 minutes, turning them after 20 minutes so they brown evenly.

Meanwhile, put the honey and sweet chilli sauce in a small saucepan. Season with salt and pepper to taste and bring to the boil. Pour the sauce over the chicken wings, mix well and let cool. Serve with radishes, if using.

sweet treats

plum pastries

You don't have to use plums and almonds to fill these easy pastries, you can use any of your favourite fruit and nuts. They can be made up to 6 hours in advance.

500 g ready-made puff pastry

12 plums, halved and pitted

8 teaspoons honey

2 tablespoons flaked almonds

2 baking sheets, lightly oiled

makes 12

Roll out the pastry on a lightly floured surface to make a large rectangle about 5 mm thick. Cut out 12 rectangles and lay well apart on the baking sheets.

Put 2 plum halves on each piece of pastry, then sprinkle with the honey and almonds.

Bake in a preheated oven at 180°C (350°F) Gas 4 for 15–20 minutes until puffed and golden. Remove from the oven and serve hot or cold.

tiramisù

Foolproof and very quick to prepare, tiramisù is the perfect pudding to serve a large group of people – it can be made in advance, doesn't need cooking or heating and tastes so delicious that it is universally welcomed. I like to make it with amaretti biscuits and present it in groovy glasses instead of one large serving bowl.

50 amaretti biscuits, crushed

200 ml Kahlúa (coffee liqueur)

6 tablespoons brandy

100 ml strong black coffee

1 kg mascarpone cheese

8 eggs, separated

100 g caster sugar, sifted

250 g dark chocolate, grated, or 4 tablespoons cocoa powder

20 glasses or a 30 cm square serving dish

serves 20

Arrange a quarter of the crushed amaretti biscuits at the bottom of the glasses or serving dish. Put the Kahlúa in a small bowl with the brandy and coffee and stir. Pour a quarter of this mixture over the crushed biscuits in the glasses or serving dish.

Put the mascarpone, egg yolks and caster sugar in a bowl and beat until smooth. Put the egg whites in a separate bowl, whisk until stiff, then gently fold them into the mascarpone mixture.

Spoon a quarter of the mixture over the biscuits. Repeat the layers 3 times, finishing with a layer of mascarpone mixture.

Sprinkle the grated chocolate or cocoa over the top of the tiramisù and refrigerate overnight. Serve chilled or at room temperature.

Top tip: Instead of topping the tiramisù with grated chocolate, melt the chocolate in the microwave in a plastic bag tied securely to close. Make a small hole in one corner and pipe 20 squiggles onto baking parchment. Let set, then insert the chocolate shapes upright into the individual glasses.

raspberries in champagne jelly

This simple but delicious combination is a refreshingly light way to round off an evening's indulgence. If champagne seems a bit decadent, use a good bottle of cava or a New World sparkling wine. These jellies can be made the day before and chilled until needed.

25 g gelatine

500 g raspberries

1 bottle champagne, at room temperature

8 glasses

serves 8

Put 3 tablespoons hot water in a small bowl and sprinkle over the gelatine. Set aside in a warm place to dissolve, about 10 minutes.

Divide the raspberries between the glasses. Open the champagne and add a little to the dissolved gelatine. Transfer to a jug and add the remaining champagne. Mix gently so that you don't build up a froth. Pour into the glasses on top of the raspberries, then chill for 2 hours, until set.

espresso granita

A refreshing end to a meal at a summer party. Good amaretti biscuits can be purchased from Italian delis and fine food stores. This granita can be made the day before and stored in the freezer until needed.

75 g sugar

9 tablespoons freshly ground coffee

to serve

amaretti biscuits

single cream (optional)

12 small glasses or espresso cups

serves 12

Put 12 small glasses or espresso cups in the freezer to chill. Put the sugar and coffee in a cafetière. Add 900 ml boiling water and let stand for 5 minutes to develop the flavour. Plunge the cafetière, pour the coffee into a heatproof jug and let cool before chilling in the refrigerator.

When very cold, pour the coffee into a bowl and freeze for about 20 minutes, until ice crystals have formed around the edge. Crush the crystals with a fork and return to the freezer. Repeat this process about 3 times until you have an even mixture of fine ice crystals.

Cover and return to the freezer until ready to serve. Serve the granita in the glasses or cups with some amaretti biscuits and a sprinkling of cream for those who prefer their coffee white.

mini chocolate brownie squares

Everyone loves brownies – rich, sticky and chocolaty, they make the perfect party treat. These are at their best if made on the day of the party, but if you are busy make them the day before and store them in an airtight container until needed.

110 g good-quality dark chocolate
(70 per cent cocoa solids)

110 g butter

2 eggs, beaten

225 g caster sugar

110 g self-raising flour

50 g pecan nuts, chopped (optional)

a rectangular cake tin, 28 x 18 cm,
lined with baking parchment

makes about 54

Put the chocolate and butter in a large saucepan and melt over low heat. Remove from the heat, add the eggs, sugar, flour and pecans, if using, and mix well. Pour into the prepared cake tin, smooth over the surface and bake in a preheated oven at 180°C (350°F) Gas 4 for 30 minutes.

Remove from the oven and let cool in the tin. When cool, lift the slab of brownies out of the tin using the baking parchment, then cut into bite-sized squares.

Top tip: If there are any brownies left over at the end of the party, they will keep for several days in an airtight container.

exotic fruit salad

Not an apple or orange in sight in this exotic fruit salad. I like it to be full of fruit from the tropics, chosen according to cost and what's in season. Include no more than four varieties, so the individual flavours will be strong and sharp.

choose from sweet pineapple, mango, papaya, bananas, lychee, fresh coconut, watermelon, melon, pomegranate, passionfruit or persimmon

freshly squeezed juice of 4 limes

serves 8

Prepare the chosen fruits, arrange on a serving dish, then squeeze the lime juice over the top. Serve with cocktail sticks or teaspoons, depending on the selection of fruit.

chocolate-dipped strawberries

Chocolate always makes a sensational dessert but here I have balanced the chocolate with fruit, in this case strawberries. Any variety of fruit can, of course, be dipped. These can be made up to 2 hours in advance.

100 g dark chocolate
100 g white chocolate
12 large strawberries

baking parchment
12 wooden skewers

serves 12

Put the dark chocolate and white chocolate in 2 separate bowls and set the bowls over 2 saucepans of simmering water. When melted, dip the pointed end of each strawberry into one of the chocolates and transfer to a sheet of baking parchment. When the chocolate is set, slide each strawberry onto a skewer and serve.

party drinks

vodka cranberry floaters

This tastes and looks heavenly. The blueberries add a colourful touch to this vodka classic.

1 shot vodka, 25 ml, chilled

125 ml cranberry juice

ice cubes, to serve

blueberries, to decorate

makes 1

Put the vodka in a tall glass and add the cranberry juice. Mix well. Add a few blueberries, then some ice cubes. Serve immediately.

pimm's cocktail

Use your own selection of fresh fruit, but orange, cucumber and mint are traditional.

500 ml Pimm's No. 1

2.25 litres lemonade

1 orange, sliced

a handful of mint sprigs

20 slices cucumber, cut lengthways

ice cubes, to serve

serves 10

Put the Pimm's, lemonade, lemon slices, mint and cucumber in a large jug. Chill for 2 hours before serving.

Serve in highball glasses with ice.

white wine fizz

1 bottle white wine, 750 ml

1 litre sparkling mineral water

1 apple, sliced

1 lemon, sliced

1 orange, sliced

1 kiwifruit, sliced

ice cubes

serves 8

Put all the ingredients in
a jug, mix and serve.

brown cow

½ bottle Kahlúa, 350 ml

1 litre milk

ice cubes

serves 8

Put all the ingredients in
a jug and mix. Alternatively,
put the Kahlúa in individual
glasses, and top with milk
and ice.

cosmopolitan

ice cubes, for shaking

8 shots Absolut-citron vodka, 25 ml each

8 shots Cointreau, 25 ml each

400 ml cranberry juice

freshly squeezed juice of 4 limes

a cocktail shaker

serves 8

Fill the shaker with ice cubes. Add the alcohol and juices and shake until well blended and chilled. Strain into 8 cocktail glasses and serve.

sea breeze

2 shots vodka, 25 ml each

125 ml cranberry juice

50 ml grapefruit juice

ice cubes, to serve

makes 1

Fill a highball glass with ice, add the vodka, then the fruit juices, stir and serve.

french 75

25 ml gin

25 ml freshly squeezed lemon juice

a dash of sugar syrup

ice cubes, for shaking

75 ml chilled champagne, plus extra to serve

a cocktail shaker

makes 1

Put the gin, lemon juice and sugar syrup in the cocktail shaker. Add the ice cubes and shake.

Pour into a champagne flute, add the champagne and top up with more champagne just before serving.

mojito

This is a fabulously refreshing drink. If you want to make it for more people, simply multiply the ingredients accordingly.

1 lime, cut into 16 pieces

enough mint tips to half-fill the glass

2 teaspoons sugar

crushed ice

50 ml dark rum

soda water, to taste (optional)

makes 1

Put the lime and mint in an old-fashioned glass, then sprinkle with sugar. Using a pestle or the back of a spoon, crush the lime, mint and sugar together until the sugar has dissolved.

Fill the glass with crushed ice, add the rum and stir briefly. Add soda water to taste, if using.

lobby dazzler

For authenticity, you should really use kumquats in this recipe. If you have difficulty finding them, use satsuma or clementine segments instead.

3–4 kumquats, quartered

2 teaspoons sugar

crushed ice

50 ml Absolut-kurant vodka

makes 1

Put the kumquats in an old-fashioned glass and sprinkle with sugar. Using a pestle or the back of a spoon, crush the kumquats and sugar until the sugar completely dissolves and all the fruit juice is released.

Fill the glass with crushed ice, add the vodka and stir briefly before serving.

bloody mary

If you want to provide some of your guests with a non-alcoholic version of this drink then you could make two jugs – one with everything and the other without the vodka.

5 lemons

200 ml vodka

7 cm white horseradish, freshly grated, or 1 tablespoon bottled horseradish

1 tablespoon Worcestershire sauce

1 teaspoon Tabasco sauce

750 ml tomato juice, well chilled

freshly ground black pepper

to serve

celery stalks, with leaves

crushed ice

serves 4

Half fill a large jug with crushed ice. Cut 1 lemon into slices and squeeze the juice from the others. Add the lemon juice and slices to the jug, together with all the other ingredients except the celery. Mix well. Serve in highball glasses with a celery stalk.

mulled wine

Warm your house and make your guests' hearts glow with this beautiful spicy drink known as *glühwein*. If making it for a big party, add more wine and sugar to the pan as the evening wears on.

2 bottles red wine, 750 ml each

8 whole cloves

2 oranges

3 tablespoons brown sugar

5 cm fresh ginger, peeled and chopped

1 cinnamon stick

½ teaspoon freshly grated nutmeg

serves 4

Pour the red wine into a medium saucepan. Push the cloves into the oranges, then cut each orange into quarters. Add to the pan, together with the sugar, ginger, cinnamon and nutmeg.

Heat the mixture to simmering point and simmer for about 10 minutes, then serve hot.

apple and mint fizz

There is something satisfyingly traditional about making your own drinks. This one is simple, refreshing and popular on hot summer days.

a large bunch of mint

2 litres apple juice

1 litre sparkling mineral water

ice cubes, to serve

makes about 3.5 litres

Reserve some of the mint leaves for serving and put the remainder in a heat-proof jug. Add 300 ml boiling water, let cool, then chill.

Transfer to a large container and add the apple juice, mineral water and ice cubes. Chop the reserved mint leaves, sprinkle over the top and serve.

ginger beer

This seems a large quantity of ginger beer but it's so easy to make and it does store well. Take care that the bottle tops are secure, as they can sometimes pop off unexpectedly.

3 unwaxed lemons

625 g unrefined caster sugar

10 cm fresh ginger, peeled and sliced

5 g cream of tartar

1 tablespoon brewer's yeast

ice, to serve

makes about 6 litres

Cut the zest off the lemons in strips, then remove and discard the white pith. Thinly slice the lemon flesh, removing all the pips. Put the lemon flesh and zest in a large bowl and add the sugar, ginger and cream of tartar. Add about 6 litres boiling water and let stand until tepid.

Sprinkle in the brewer's yeast and stir. Cover with clingfilm and let stand in a warm place for 24 hours. Using a large metal spoon, skim off the yeast, then strain the mixture through a sieve, discarding any sediment. Pour into bottles, then leave for 2 days before drinking. Serve chilled with ice.

melon and strawberry juice

These summer fruits, now available all year round, make a delicious, refreshing drink. This is so quick to make, you can do so just before your guests arrive.

1 melon, such as cantaloupe or honeydew, peeled and deseeded

200 g strawberries, hulled

freshly squeezed juice of 2 limes

8 ice cubes, plus extra to serve

serves 4

Chop the melon flesh into small pieces and put in a blender. Add the strawberries, lime juice and ice. Blend until smooth and serve in a large chilled jug.

Top tip: For a flavoured yoghurt drink, add natural yoghurt to the blender with the strawberries and lime juice.

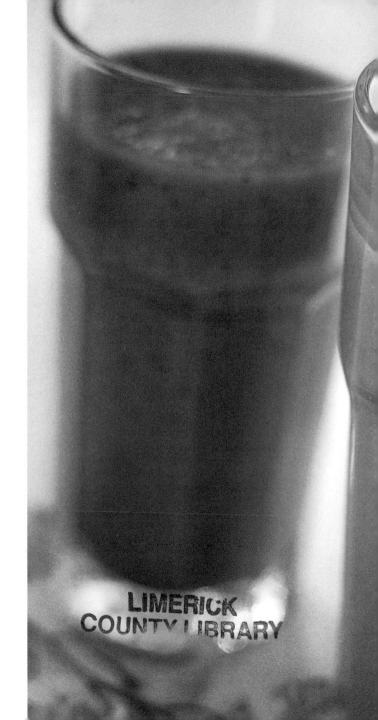

index